SALADS

Colophon

© 2003 Rebo International b.v., Lisse, The Netherlands

www.rebo-publishers.com - info@rebo-publishers.com

Original recipes and photographs: © R&R Publishing Pty. Ltd.

Design, layout and typesetting: R&R Publishing Pty. Ltd., Victoria, Australia

Cover design: Minkowsky Graphics, Enkhuizen, The Netherlands

Proofreading: Sandy Chen

ISBN 90 366 1606 9

SALADS

the most delicious side dishes
and entrees for

creative cooking

REBO
PUBLISHERS

Foreword

Salads are so delicious and versatile: keep them small for delicious side dishes, or add all sorts of tasty morsels to turn them into a main meal. Drawing inspiration from the recipes in this book, you can easilz prepare the perfect salad. How about a refreshing *Watercress and Pear Salad*, or an *Oriental Salad of Crispy Bok Choy*? Even more exotic is the *Avocado* and *Papaya Salad with Mango*, and the *Armenian Salad with Stuffed Tomatoes*. At the right time of year, a *Chef's Autumn Salad* or a *Summer Salad with Chive Dressing* only takes a moment.

Abbreviations

All measurements conform to European and American measurement systems. For easier cooking, the American cup measurement is used throughout the book.

tbsp = tablespoon

tsp = teaspoon

oz = ounce

lb = pound

°F = degrees Fahrenheit

°C = degrees Celsius

g = gram

kg = kilogram

cm = centimeter

ml = mililiter

l = liter

Method

To make the dressing: peel the mango, slice the flesh off the pit, then chop roughly. Blend to a thin purée with the vinegar, lime juice, oil, ginger, and honey in a food processor. Alternatively, press the mango flesh through a sieve, then mix with the other dressing ingredients.

Halve and peel the avocados, discard the pits, then finely slice lengthways. Toss in the lime juice to keep them from turning brown.

Halve the papayas, then scoop out and discard the seeds. Peel and finely slice the flesh. Arrange on serving plates with the avocados and salad leaves. Pour over the dressing and garnish with coriander.

Ingredients

2 ripe avocados

2 papayas

juice of ¹/₂ lime

2oz/50g mixed salad leaves

fresh coriander to garnish

Dressing

1 ripe mango

1 tbsp rice wine vinegar or

1 tsp white wine vinegar

juice of 1 lime

¹/₂ tsp sesame oil

¹/₂in/1cm piece fresh root ginger, finely chopped

¹/₂ tsp clear honey

Avocado, Mango, and Papaya Salad

Method

Preheat the oven to 350°F/180°C.

Wash and trim the beets at root and stem ends, but do not peel. In a small bowl, mix together the brown sugar, salt, rosemary and the 3 tablespoons of olive oil until well-blended, then add the whole beets and toss in the oil mixture, making sure that the beet skins are shiny.

Wrap each beetroot in foil and place in a baking dish, then roast for approximately 1 hour or until just tender. Peel the beet and cut into thick slices.

Slice the fennel bulb very finely and peel the oranges, removing any seeds. Cut the orange into segments.

To make the dressing: Combine the dill, balsamic vinegar, olive oil, and salt and pepper to taste and whisk well until thick.

Arrange the beets on a serving platter with the thinly sliced fennel and orange. Drizzle over the dill vinaigrette, then scatter the crushed hazelnuts on top.

Ingredients

5 large beetroots

1 bulb fennel

3 blood oranges

1 tbsp brown sugar

1 tsp salt

30g chopped fresh rosemary

3 tbsp olive oil

5oz/150g toasted hazelnuts, crushed

Dressing

½ cup/4 oz/120g chopped dill

2 tbsp balsamic vinegar

½ cup olive oil

salt and pepper to taste

Roasted Beet, Orange, and Fennel Salad

Method

Steam, boil, or microwave the beans until bright green and crisp-tender (do not overcook), drain well and refresh in cold water, then cut in half diagonally.

Place them in a large bowl and add the drained and rinsed chickpeas, quartered artichoke hearts, finely sliced Spanish onion, grated carrot, parsley, coriander, and dill. Stir to combine thoroughly.

Whisk the vinegar, olive oil, garlic, mustard, cumin, lemon juice, and salt and pepper in a jug. When emulsified (thick), pour over the vegetable mixture and toss very well to coat the vegetables in the dressing.

Sprinkle with toasted hazelnuts and serve.

Ingredients

1lb 5oz/600g green beans

14 oz/2 x 400g cans chickpeas

8 x preserved artichoke hearts, quartered (either in water or oil)

1 small Spanish onion, peeled and very finely sliced

1 medium carrot, grated

1/2 cup/4 oz/120g chopped parsley

1/2 cup/4 oz/120g chopped coriander

2 tbsp/1oz/30g fresh dill

2 tbsp white wine vinegar

3 tbsp olive oil

1 clove garlic, minced

1 tsp mustard

1 tsp ground cumin

juice of 1 large lemon

3 1/2 oz/100g toasted hazelnuts, chopped

salt and pepper to taste

Middle Eastern Bean and Artichoke Salad

Method

To make the dressing: place the oil, apple juice, vinegar, mustard, garlic, herbs, and black pepper in a bowl, then whisk with a fork to mix thoroughly.

Pour the dressing over the mushrooms and stir well. Cover and place in the fridge for 2 hours.

Arrange the spinach and watercress on serving plates. Spoon the mushrooms and a little of the dressing over the top and toss lightly to mix. Garnish with fresh thyme.

Marinated Mushrooms on a Bed of Leaves

Ingredients

12oz/350g mixed mushrooms, such as shitake, large open, button, or oyster, thickly sliced

3½ oz/100g baby spinach leaves

1oz/25g watercress,

thick stems discarded

fresh thyme to garnish

Dressing

3 tbsp extra virgin olive oil

2 tbsp unsweetened apple juice

2 tsp tarragon

white wine vinegar

2 tsp Dijon mustard

1 clove garlic, crushed

1 tbsp mixed chopped fresh herbs; choose from oregano, thyme, chives, basil or parsley

black pepper

salads

Method

Wash the beets and scrub them until clean. If your beets have their greens attached, remove them and set aside. Trim the bottom if necessary, but be careful not to cut the beetr itself.

Toss the beetroots and olive oil together, then place them in a baking dish. Cover with foil or a lid and roast at 400°F/200°C for 30-45 minutes or until tender.

Remove the beets from the oven and cool, then peel the skin away and discard. Cut the beets in half lengthways and add salt and pepper to taste.

Wash the greens thoroughly meanwhile to remove all traces of sand and grit. Heat the butter in a sauté pan and add the greens, tossing for 1 minute until wilted. Remove the greens, add the balsamic vinegar and bring to a boil, whisking in the butter. Return the peeled beets and toss them in the vinegar until there is a shiny sheer on the reduced beets.

Transfer the beets to a platter or bowl and arrange with the wilted beet leaves. Scatter over the dill and roasted hazelnuts, adding small dollops of the sour cream or yogurt, if desired. Add black pepper to taste.

Ingredients

24 very small beets, greens attached if possible

1 tbsp olive oil

salt and freshly ground pepper to taste

1 tbsp butter

2 tbsp balsamic vinegar

3 tbsp fresh dill, snipped

2 tbsp sour cream or yogurt (optional)

3½ oz/100g hazelnuts, roasted and chopped

black pepper to taste

Roasted Beet Salad with Balsamic and Dill

Method

Slice the cabbage finely and mix in a large bowl with the sliced bok choy, julienne spring onions, water chestnuts, julienne carrots, and finely sliced lemon grass and lime leaves. Toss thoroughly.

Whisk together all the dressing ingredients in a jug until smooth and well-seasoned, then pour over the salad ingredients and toss thoroughly until all the vegetables are coated with the dressing.

Mix through the coriander at the last minute and sprinkle with the crushed peanuts or sunflower seeds; serve immediately.

Ingredients

½ large curly cabbage, very finely sliced 4 baby bok choy, leaves separated and sliced

8 spring onions, julienned lengthways

7oz/200g can sliced water chestnuts, drained

2 medium carrots, finely julienned

2 stalks lemon grass, very finely sliced

4 kaffir lime leaves, very finely sliced

Dressing

2 tbsp low fat mayonnaise

2 tbsp low fat yogurt

juice of 2 lemons

juice of 1 lime

1 tbsp freshly grated ginger

4 tbsp rice vinegar

salt and pepper to taste

Asian Gingered Coleslaw

Garnish

1 bunch of coriander, well washed and roughly chopped;

½ cup of toasted peanuts or sunflower seeds.

Method

Soak the black cloud fungus for 15 minutes then drain. Rinse the soaked mushrooms thoroughly in cold water If using dried shiitake, soak in hot water for 15 minutes then drain and slice. If using fresh shiitake, slice finely.

Place the shredded chicken in a large bowl. Break up the cooked noodles under hot running water until the noodles have separated, then shake off excess water and add to the chicken. Add the mushrooms, sliced snow peas, well-washed baby bok choy leaves, diced pepper, sliced spring onions, and water chestnuts and toss well.

Whisk together the ginger, yoghurt, kecap manis, hoisin, mirin, rice vinegar, sweet chili, fish sauce, lime juice and salt and pepper to taste in a jug. Add to the chicken salad and toss well until all the ingredients are coated. Garnish with the toasted slivered almonds and chopped chervil and serve.

Ingredients

8 fresh or dried shiitake mushrooms

1/3oz/10g black cloud mushrooms

4 cups shredded skinless cooked chicken, about 28oz/800g

1lb/2 x 500g packets fresh Asian hokkien noodles

7 oz/200g fresh snow peas, sliced diagonally

4 baby bok choy, well-washed and leaves separated

1 diced red pepper

4 spring onions, finely sliced

8oz/250g can sliced water chestnuts, drained

1 tbsp freshly minced ginger

1/4 cup/2oz/60g plain low fat yogurt

3 tbsp kecap manis (Indonesian sweet soy)

1 tbsp hoisin sauce (Chinese barbecue sauce)

3 tbsp mirin (sweet Japanese rice wine)

3 tbsp rice vinegar

3 tbsp sweet chilli sauce

1 tbsp fish sauce

juice of 1 lime

salt and pepper to taste

2 tbsp slivered almonds, toasted

1 bunch of chervil (or parsley or coriander)

Asian Chicken Bok Choy Salad

Method

Blanch the snow peas, asparagus, and sugar snap peas in boiling water for 30 seconds, drain and refresh in a bowl of iced cold water. Drain well.

Cook peas in boiling water for 5 minutes, or until tender, drain and refresh in iced water. Drain well. Combine all vegetables and cherry tomatoes.

To make the dressing: whisk all ingredients until well-combined and toss over vegetables and serve.

Summer Greens with Lime and Coriander

Ingredients

	Dressing
8oz/250g snow peas, topped and tailed	
2 bunches asparagus, cut in half	2 tbsp lime juice
8oz/250g sugar snap, topped and tailed	3 tbsp chopped coriander
8oz/250g fresh peas (shelled)	½ cup olive oil
½ box cherry tomatoes, cut in half	1 tbsp white wine vinegar

salads

Method

Preheat the grill to high. Lay the bacon slices flat on the grill rack, then cook for 4-5 minutes on each side, until crispy. Remove and set aside for 5 minutes to cool. Chop or crumble into small pieces.

Put the salad leaves into a large bowl or onto a large platter, then scatter the sliced mushrooms and peppers over the top. Add the tomato quarters and the Gruyère matchsticks. Scatter over the bacon pieces and season with salt and pepper.

To make the dressing: put the vinegar, mustard and oil into a jug or screwtop jar and stir or shake well to combine. Stir in the snipped chives, pour the dressing over the salad and serve.

Ingredients

4oz/125g smoked bacon

4oz/130g bag mixed salad leaves

3oz/75g mushrooms, sliced thinly

1 green or yellow pepper, halved,

deseeded and thinly sliced

4 tomatoes, quartered

4oz/125g Gruyère cheese, cut into matchsticks

salt and black pepper

For the dressing

1 tbsp wine vinegar

1 tsp French mustard

4 tbsp olive oil

1 tbsp snipped fresh chives

Summer Salad with Chive Dressing

Method

Prepare the noodles first. Fill a deep jug or bowl with very warm water and soak the cellophane noodles for about 10 minutes or until they are soft and tender. Drain. Mix together the fish sauce, rice vinegar, 2 tablespoons of mirin and sugar, then toss through the cellophane noodles. Add the coriander, mix well, and set aside.

Heat the peanut oil in a wok and add the ginger, chili, garlic, and spring onions and toss thoroughly until the spring onions have wilted, about 3 minutes. Add the broccoli florets and toss well until bright green. Add the mushrooms and corn and continue tossing over high heat. Add the soy sauce, 3 tablespoons of mirin, and rice vinegar and continue cooking for 1 minute.

Add the noodles and mix well, then remove the pan from the heat.

Divide the shredded lettuce amongst the plates, then top with the broccoli noodle mixture. Garnish with toasted almonds and fresh, chopped coriander.

Ingredients

Salad

1 tbsp peanut oil

1 tbsp grated fresh ginger

1 very finely sliced small hot red chili

4 cloves garlic, minced

4 spring onions, minced

10 fresh shiitake mushrooms, sliced

1lb/500g broccoli florets, trimmed

7oz/200g baby corn

3 tbsp soy sauce

3 tbsp mirin, extra

2 tbsp rice vinegar

1 head lettuce, shredded

4oz/120g blanched almonds, toasted

coriander, extra, for garnish

Gingered Almond Broccoli Salad
with Cellophane Noodles

Noodles

3¹/₂oz/100g dried cellophane noodles

2 tbsp fish sauce

2 tbsp rice vinegar

2 tbsp mirin (sweet Japanese rice wine)

1 tsp palm or brown sugar

¹/₂ cup/4 oz/125g chopped fresh coriander

Method

Wash and dry the spinach. Remove the fibrous stems and center leaf veins. Slice the onion and eggs into rings. Mix all the ingredients together and toss with the dressing.

To make the dressing: combine the sour cream and onion until smooth in a blender and set aside in the refrigerator for at least 2 hours. Add the vinegar and season with salt and pepper.

Spinach Salad

Ingredients

1lb/500g young spinach

1 large Spanish onion

3 hard-boiled eggs

5 oz/155g black olives

Dressing

¼ cup sour cream

1 medium onion, chopped

1 tbsp red wine vinegar

salt and pepper

Method

Cut the bread into cubes and toss with 2 tablespoons olive oil and the rosemary. Spread onto a baking tray and bake at 400°F/200°C for 5 minutes until golden, then allow to cool.

To make the dressing: heat a heavy pan and brush the skins of the small tomatoes with a little olive oil. Cook the whole tomatoes in the pan until well-blackened all over. Purèe with the remaining olive oil, vinegars, garlic, and salt and pepper to taste. Set aside.

Remove the seeds from the other tomatoes and chop into small chunks. Peel the cucumber and remove the seeds with a spoon. Finely chop the Spanish onion. Remove the seeds from the olives by squashing them with the wide blade of a knife.

Place the bread cubes, tomatoes, cucumber, Spanish onion, olives, and torn basil leaves into a mixing bowl. Add the chopped mint and marjoram. Mix well. Pour the dressing over and toss thoroughly. Allow to sit for 10 minutes, then serve.

Ingredients

1lb 5oz/600g stale, rustic Italian-style bread (about ½ loaf)

2 tbsp olive oil

2 tbsp fresh rosemary, chopped

2lb/1kg assorted tomatoes

1 continental cucumber

1 small Spanish onion

20 kalamata olives

20 basil leaves

4 mint leaves, finely sliced

1 tbsp fresh marjoram

Dressing

4 small tomatoes

½ cup quality olive oil

2 tbsp red wine vinegar

1 tbsp balsamic vinegar

3 cloves garlic

salt and freshly ground pepper

Tuscan Panzanella with Roasted Tomato Vinaigrette

Method

Note: Salads such as this one are perfect summer accompaniments to meat, chicken or fish dishes but also make wonderful entrées. This dish is full of robust flavours and is even lovely as part of an antipasto platter.

Cover the potatoes in cold water and boil all the way through until just tender, about 15-20min. Drain and leave aside until just cool enough to handle, then peel and slice thinly.

Cut the tomatoes in half and remove the hard inner core. Slice the tomatoes and add them to the potatoes. Add the finely sliced Spanish onions and toss well.

Add the basil leaves, oregano, olive oil, vinegar, and add a little salt and pepper. Toss everything carefully and serve at once.

Ingredients

4 fist-sized unpeeled potatoes, scrubbed and washed

8 firm Roma tomatoes

3 Spanish onions, peeled and sliced thinly,

then soaked in cold water for 30 minutes

15 small, whole, fresh basil leaves

1 heaping tsp dried oregano

4 tbsp olive oil

3 tbsp white or red wine vinegar

salt and pepper to taste

Calabrian Salad

salads

Method

Bring a large saucepan of lightly salted water to a boil. Add the leeks, and peas and cook for 2 minutes, then add the mangetout and stir for a few seconds. Drain and set aside.

Add 2 tablespoons of oil to the pan, then add the garlic and spring onions. Stir for a minute to soften slightly, then put in the spinach and stir until it starts to wilt. Put the rest of the cooked vegetables in the pan with the remaining oil. Lightly season and fry for 2 minutes to heat through.

Add the ham to the pan and heat through for 1-2 minutes. Arrange the mixture on a serving plate. Scatter over the mushrooms and sprinkle with lemon juice. Shave over the Parmesan, if using, and season with black pepper.

Ingredients

salt and black pepper

2 leeks, white parts only, sliced

7oz/200g garden peas

5oz/150g mangetout

3 tbsp olive oil

1 clove garlic, thinly sliced

3 shallots, cut into 2in/5cm lengths

3oz/75g baby spinach

3 slices Serrano ham, cut into thin slices

2 large mushrooms, very thinly sliced

few drops of lemon juice

Parmesan to serve (optional)

Warm Vegetable Salad with Serrano Ham

Method

Wash and dry the watercress well.

Whisk the olive oil, lemon juice and white wine vinegar with salt and pepper until the mixture has thickened slightly.

Slice the pears finely and combine with watercress in a bowl.

Drizzle over dressing just enough to coat the leaves. Place on a platter and top with shavings of Parmesan.

Watercress and Pear Salad

Ingredients

2 bunches of watercress, picked and washed

3 tbsp olive oil

1 tbsp lemon juice

½ tbsp white wine vinegar

3 bosc pears, finely sliced

shavings of Parmesan

salt and pepper

Method

Combine the shredded carrots, raisins, and pecans in a bowl. Moisten with dressing made by shaking the ingredients together in a screw-top jar. Serve on washed and crisp lettuce leaves on individual plates or on one serving dish.

Note: This is a variation of a popular French salad - carrot and walnut. Pecans are used in place of the walnuts as they keep better.

Ingredients

8 oz/250g carrots, shredded

3oz/90g raisins

6-8 pecan halves, chopped

1 head romaine lettuce

Dressing

2 tbsp olive oil

2 tsp hazelnut or walnut oil (optional)

1 tbsp lemon juice

salt and pepper

Carrot & Pecan Salad

Method

To make the marinade: mix together the soy sauce, honey, and sesame oil, if using. Place the chicken in a non-metallic bowl and pour over the marinade. Toss the chicken well to coat, then cover and refrigerate for 30 minutes.

Heat 1 tablespoon of the peanut oil and 1 tablespoon of the sesame oil in a wok or large, heavy-based frying pan. Add the chicken and stir-fry for 5-6 minutes, until cooked through and browned. Remove from the pan and leave to cool.

Add the remaining oil, garlic, chili and ginger to the pan and fry, stirring and scraping the bottom of the pan, for 3-4 minutes, until the garlic starts to brown.

Stir in the vinegar and 5 tablespoons of water, then bring to a boil and remove from the heat.

Arrange the salad leaves on plates, top with the chicken strips and spoon over the warm dressing.

Marinated Chicken Salad with Warm Dressing

Ingredients

4 skinless, boneless chicken breasts,

cut into ½in/1cm strips

2 tbsp peanut oil

2 tbsp sesame oil

2 cloves garlic, chopped

1-2 red or green chilies,

deseeded and finely sliced

1in/2.5cm piece fresh root ginger, finely grated

²/₅ cup red wine vinegar

3oz/2 x 80g bags herb salad

Marinade

2 tbsp dark soy sauce

2 tbsp clear honey

1 tbsp sesame oil (optional)

Method

Peel the oranges over a small bowl to reserve the juice, using a small, sharp knife. Cut the flesh into segments and place in a separate bowl.

Stir in the cooked, shredded chicken, celery, spring onions and yellow pepper, then season well. Meanwhile, make the dressing by mixing all the ingredients together, including the reserved orange juice, in a small bowl until well-combined.

Arrange the salad leaves and chicken mixture between four plates and pour over the dressing.

Ingredients

2 oranges

2 chicken breast fillets, cooked and shredded

2 celery sticks, cut into fine strips

2 spring onions, finely shredded

1 yellow pepper, deseeded
and cut into fine strips

sea salt and freshly ground
black pepper

2 x 120g packs Alfresco salad

Dressing

$^2/_3$ cup natural yogurt

2 tbsp mayonnaise

2 tsp clear honey

1 tbsp roughly chopped fresh parsley

Chicken and Orange Salad

Method

Bring a large saucepan of salted water to a boil. Add the broccoli, return to a boil, then cook for 1-2 minutes, until slightly softened. Drain and leave to cool for 15 minutes. Meanwhile, make the dressing. Mix together the mustard, lime juice, yogurt, oil, coriander, and seasoning.

Place the lettuce, red onion, cucumber, broccoli, celery, carrots, and apples in a large bowl. Pour over the dressing and toss to coat. Arrange the turkey or ham slices in the center of a shallow serving dish or platter and spoon the salad around the edge. Scatter over the raisins and peanuts, if using.

Ingredients

salt and black pepper

8oz/225g broccoli, cut into small florets

1 romaine lettuce, leaves torn

1 red onion, halved and sliced

$\frac{1}{2}$ cucumber, peeled and sliced

2 sticks celery, sliced

2 carrots, cut into matchsticks

2 apples, sliced

8 oz/200g wafer-thin cooked turkey or ham slices

2 tbsp raisins

roasted salted peanuts

Dressing

1 tsp Dijon mustard

juice of $\frac{1}{2}$ lime

5 oz/150g carton low fat natural yogurt

2 tbsp olive oil

1 tbsp chopped fresh coriander

Autumn Chef's Salad

Method

Place the salad leaves in a large bowl, then make the dressing. Mix the oil, vinegar, lemon juice, mustard, and honey together, then set aside.

Cut the chicken livers into large pieces, removing any fibrous bits. Heat the oil and butter in a large heavy-based frying pan. Add the livers, fresh herbs, garlic and seasoning, then cook over a medium to high heat for 5-8 minutes, until browned on all sides. Remove the livers and place on top of the salad.

Pour the dressing into the pan, stir vigorously to mix with the pan juices and cook for 3 minutes or until reduced slightly. Pour the dressing over the salad, toss well and serve.

Warm Chicken Liver Salad

Ingredients

7oz/200g bag mixed salad leaves

9oz/2 x 250g packs frozen chicken livers, defrosted

1 tbsp olive oil

2 tbsp butter

2 tbsp chopped mixed fresh herbs, such as flat-leaf

parsley, sage, marjoram, or thyme

2 cloves garlic, crushed

salt and black pepper

Dressing

6 tbsp olive oil

1 tbsp wine vinegar

juice of 1 lemon

2 tsp Dijon mustard

2 tsp clear honey

Method

Make the marinade: Ground 2 tablespoons of the mustard seeds into powder, then mix the ground seeds with the malt vinegar, honey, molasses, brown sugar, olive oil, French mustard, garlic, and boiling water. Whisk until mixture is thick and smooth.

Reserve 4 tablespoons of marinade for later. Lay the chicken in a flat glass dish and pour over the remaining marinade. Turn the chicken so that both sides are covered in the marinade and chill for a minimum of 4 hours.

Remove the chicken from the marinade, making sure that each piece of chicken has a good coating of the marinade. Place in an ovenproof baking dish or oven tray and bake at 410°F/210°C for 20-25 minutes, until cooked through.

Transfer the reserved marinade to a saucepan and bring to a boil. Simmer for 5 minutes, then remove from the heat. Remove the chicken from the oven and keep warm.

Make a dressing out of the red or white wine vinegar and olive oil with salt and pepper to taste and a little of the reserved marinade. Whisk well. Toss some dressing through the mixed lettuce and spinach leaves just to coat. Add the shallots and chives and toss again.

Arrange the salad leaves on plates, then top each mound of salad with a chicken breast, sliced diagonally. Drizzle with remaining warm marinade.

Ingredients

3 tbsp mustard seeds

3 tbsp malt vinegar

2 tbsp honey

1 tbsp molasses

1 tbsp brown sugar

½ cup olive oil

4 tbsp French mustard

2 cloves garlic, minced

½ cup boiling water

8 skinless chicken breast fillets

2 tbsp red or white wine vinegar

2 tbsp olive oil

salt and pepper to taste

Warm Salad of Mustard-glazed Chicken with Red Wine Vinaigrette

10¹/₂ oz/300g assorted baby lettuce leaves (mesclun), well-washed and dried

10¹/₂ oz/300g baby spinach leaves, well-washed and dried

1 bunch shallots, sliced on the diagonally

1 bunch chives, chopped

Method

Heat the oven to 370°F/190°C. Season duck breast with a little salt and pepper. Heat peanut oil in a pan until almost smoking, then add the duck breast, skin side down, and cook on a high heat until the skin is a deep caramel brown. Transfer the pan with duck to the preheated oven and cook until the duck is cooked rare, 7-10 minutes. (Do not turn the duck breasts over.)

Remove the pan from the oven and remove the breasts from pan, keeping them warm, then drain and discard the excess fat. Add the butter and when it begins to bubble, add the thyme leaves and the honey. When simmering, replace duck breasts, skin side up.

Cook for a further minute on low heat, then remove pan altogether. Whisk together the lemon juice, walnut oil, salt and pepper and the pan juices and mix well. Toss the lettuce leaves and pomegranate through a little of the dressing.

Divide the lettuce leaves between the plates, garnish with tomatoes. Slice the duck breast and arrange around the salad, drizzling any excess honey sauce over the duck slices. Garnish with basil leaves and serve.

Salad of Sautéed Duck with Thyme and Honey

Ingredients

3 duck breasts, skin-on

salt and pepper

1 tbsp peanut oil

2 tsp butter

1 sprig thyme, leaves picked from the stalk

2 tbsp honey

1 tbsp lemon juice

2 tbsp walnut oil

fine grey sea salt and cracked black pepper

7oz/200g mixed mesclun, washed and spun dry

1 pomegranate (optional), seeds and pulp scooped out

6 large cherry tomatoes

basil leaves to garnish

Method

Slice the tomatoes in half lengthways, and top with sliced basil, mint, salt, pepper, and sugar. Bake at 320°F/160°C for 2 hours.

Whisk together all the dressing ingredients until emulsified (thickened) in a large jug.

Marinate the chicken in ½ cup of dressing, reserving the remainder for later. Allow the chicken to marinate for at least an hour (or up to 4 hours). Heat a non stick grill pan and cook the chicken fillets over a high heat until cooked through, 2-3 minutes on each side.

Transfer the cooked fillets to a plate and keep warm. Steam, microwave, or boil the asparagus until tender, then refresh under cold water. Halve the avocado, peel, and dice the flesh. Slice the spring onions diagonally and thinly slice the mushrooms. Dice the mango flesh.

To make the salad: place the well-washed spinach leaves in a large bowl and add the blanched asparagus, sliced shallots, mushrooms and roasted tomatoes, cut into quarters. Add the reserved dressing and toss thoroughly.

Divide the salad evenly amongst individual plates and add some mango and avocado cubes. Top with 2 chicken fillets, and a generous sprinkling of nut medley. Serve immediately.

Ingredients

Salad

6 Roma tomatoes

10 basil leaves

10 mint leaves

½ tsp sugar

12 tiny chicken fillets (from breasts)

1 bunch of asparagus

1 avocado

salt and pepper

1 bunch shallots

8 firm button mushrooms

2 firm mangoes

3 large handfuls of baby spinach leaves

½ cup/4oz/120g toasted hazelnuts, lightly crushed

½ cup/4oz/120g toasted brazil nuts, lightly crushed

½ cup/4oz/120g toasted pistachios, lightly crushed

Summer Salad of Grilled Chicken, Spinach, and Mango

Dressing

2 tsp honey

2 tbsp balsamic vinegar

3 tbsp raspberry vinegar

2 tbsp soy sauce

2 tsp Dijon mustard

2 tsp minced ginger

2 cloves garlic, minced

1 tsp sambal oelek (chili paste)

2 tbsp lemon juice

2 tbsp olive oil (optional)

salt and freshly ground pepper

salads

Method

Bring a small saucepan of water to a boil, then the eggs and boil for 10 minutes. Remove from the pan, cool under cold running water, then shell. Cut each egg lengthways into quarters.

Arrange 8 alternating chicory and lettuce leaves, tips facing outwards, in a star shape on each serving plate. Place 2 egg quarters on the base of 2 opposite lettuce leaves, then place 2 anchovy halves on the other 2 opposite lettuce leaves. Scatter the capers over the leaves.

Place a cherry tomato half on the center of each plate and drape 2 anchovy halves over the top. Shave over the Parmesan, using a vegetable peeler, then drizzle over the olive oil and lemon juice. Season to taste and garnish with parsley.

Anchovy, Egg, and Parmesan Salad

Ingredients

3 medium eggs

2 heads chicory

2 little Gem lettuce, leaves torn

12 anchovy fillets in oil, drained and cut in half lengthways

1 tbsp capers, drained

3 cherry tomatoes, halved

2oz Parmesan

3 tbsp extra virgin olive oil

Juice of 1/2 lemon

salt and black pepper

fresh flat-leaf parsley to garnish

Method

Grate 1 teaspoon of grapefruit rind finely and reserve for the dressing. Slice the top and bottom off of each grapefruit, then cut off the peel and pith, following the curve of the fruit. Cut between the membranes to release the segments and reserve.

To make the dressing: place the mayonnaise in a bowl, then stir in the vinegar, ketchup, Tabasco, and Worcestershire sauce to taste. Stir in the grated grapefruit rind, tarragon, and sour cream, then season.

Arrange the lettuce in serving bowls. Set aside.

Reserve some shrimp in the shell for garnish, but shell the remainder. Rinse and dry on kitchen towels, then mix with grapefruit segments and heap onto the lettuce. Spoon over the dressing, sprinkle with paprika, then garnish with the unpeeled. Serve with lemon wedges.

Ingredients

2 pink or ruby red grapefruits

2 heads little Gem or romaine lettuce, shredded

1lb/450g large cooked shell-on shrimp, defrosted if frozen

paprika for dusting

lemon wedges to serve

Dressing

6 tbsp mayonnaise

1 tbsp tarragon white wine vinegar

2 tbsp tomato ketchup

Few drops Tabasco sauce (optional)

1-2 tsp Worcestershire sauce

2 tsp chopped fresh tarragon

2 tbsp sour cream

salt and black pepper

Shrimp and Grapefruit Cocktail

Method

To make the dressing: place the tomatoes in a bowl and cover with boiling water. Leave for 30 seconds, then skin, deseed, and cut into. Whisk together the oil and vinegar in a bowl, then whisk in the cream, tarragon small pieces and seasoning. Add sugar and Worcestershire sauce to taste, then stir in the tomatoes and cucumber.

Mix together the crabmeat and sliced fennel and stir in 4 tablespoons of the dressing. Arrange the salad leaves together with the crab mixture on plates. Spoon over the remaining dressing, then sprinkle with the chives, chopped fennel top, and paprika or cayenne pepper.

Ingredients

2 large dressed crabs (about 9oz/250g crabmeat)

1 large bulb fennel, thinly sliced, and feathery top

chopped and reserved for garnish

3oz/80g bag mixed salad leaves

1 tbsp/15g snipped fresh chives

and paprika or cayenne pepper to garnish

Crab Salad with Tomato Dressing

Dressing

2 large tomatoes

5 tbsp olive oil

1 tbsp white wine vinegar

4 tbs plight cream

1 tsp chopped fresh tarragon

salt and black pepper

pinch of caster sugar

dash of Worcestershire sauce

2in piece cucumber, diced

Method

Cut the fish into 1cm/½in cubes and mix with ¾ cup of the lime juice, half the coconut milk, salt and pepper to taste. Stir well and marinate overnight or for at least 4 hours. When the fish is firm and looks opaque (cooked), drain away and discard the liquid.

Mix the drained fish with the pepper slices, chili and tomato.

Add the remaining coconut milk and lime juice and stir to combine thoroughly.

Serve cold in glasses with wedges of lime or lemon as an entrée.

Ingredients

3½ lb/1.5kg firm white fish

1 cup fresh lime juice (or lemon juice)

10oz/300ml can coconut milk

1 small red pepper, finely diced

1 small green pepper, finely diced

1 small red chili, minced

1 firm tomato, finely diced

lime or lemon wedges, for garnish

salt and pepper to taste

Fijian Kokoda

Method

Cook the rice by the absorption method (p. 10) with the saffron. Spread out to cool. Put all the salad ingredients into a bowl and mix well. Combine the dressing ingredients in a cruet jar and shake well. Pour the dressing over the salad and mix gently.

Serve on a bed of tender lettuce leaves. Reserve some of the strips of pepper, olives, and shrimp to garnish the rice.

Spanish Shrimp Salad

Ingredients

2 cups long-grain rice

grated peel of 1/2 lemon

1 cup black olives, pitted

18oz/500 g cooked shrimp

Dressing

2 tbsp chopped basil or parsley

3 cups water

3 red peppers cut into strips

4 tbsp olive oil

lettuce leaves for serving

1/2 tsp saffron threads, soaked in

3 tomatoes, peeled and diced

2 tsp warm water

salt and pepper

1 tbsp lemon juice

Method

Cook the eggs in simmering water for about 7 minutes, add the green beans and cook for a further 3 minutes. Drain, and set the green beans aside; shell and quarter the eggs, then set aside.

Wash, and wipe the fish fillets with kitchen paper then place in a shallow frying pan. Cover with water and bring to a boil, simmer for 5 minutes. Remove from the heat and let sit for 5 minutes or until cooked and beginning to flake. Drain the fish, skin, then flake into pieces.

To make the dressing: combine all the ingredients together in a small bowl. Heat 2in/5cm of oil in a frying pan over a high heat, and fry the potatoes for 5-6 minutes until golden and crisp. Drain on kitchen paper and season with salt.

Combine the beans, eggs, flaked salmon, onion, cherry tomatoes and dressing in a large bowl.

Arrange the salad leaves on plates, place the salmon on top with the potatoes, garnish with basil leaves and serve.

Ingredients

3 medium eggs

3oz/75g green beans, chopped

3 salmon fillets

sunflower oil, for deep frying

8oz/225g baby new potatoes, sliced very thinly

1 small red onion, finely sliced

4oz/125g cherry

tomatoes, halved

4oz/120g pack Alfresco salad

fresh basil leaves, to garnish

Dressing

4 tbsp olive oil

2 tsp red wine vinegar

2 tsp balsamic vinegar

1 garlic clove, crushed

sea salt and freshly

ground black pepper

Warm Salmon Salad

Method

Combine mince, coriander, fish and chilli sauce, and flour, mix well.

Shape into small balls, chill for 30 minutes.

Place noodles in a large bowl and cover with boiling water. Leave until soft,

approximately 30 minutes.

Combine dressing ingredients in a cruet.

Heat oil and cook pork balls 8-10 minutes, turn to brown, remove.

Combine noodles, pork, carrot, pour over dressing and toss well. Serve.

Ingredients	Dressing
1lb 2oz/500g lean pork mince	1 bunch coriander, finely chopped
3 tbs fresh coriander, finely chopped	1 tbs grated ginger
2 tsp/10ml fish sauce	1 Spanish (red) onion, thinly sliced
2 tbs sweet chilli sauce	1-2 red chillies, finely chopped
1 tbs flour	2 tsp brown sugar
1 tbs oil	½ cup fresh lime juice
10oz/300g vermicelli (cellophane) noodles	2 tbs fish sauce
1 large carrot, cut into thin strips	1½ tbs peanut oil

Salad of Pork and Vermicelli Noodles

Method

Slice the tops off the tomatoes, and scoop out as much flesh as possible without damaging the exterior of the tomato. Chop the tomato pulp finely.

Heat the olive oil and cook the chopped onion and leek until slightly golden. Add the rice, tomato pulp, nuts, currants, parsley, mint, salt and pepper and sautè until the mixture is hot and well-flavored.

Fill each tomato with the rice mixture and replace the tops of the tomatoes.

Combine the garlic, stock, and white wine and drizzle around tomatoes. Bake at 350°F/180°C for 15 minutes.

Wash and dry the spinach leaves meanwhile. When the tomatoes have finished cooking, remove them and toss the remaining hot liquid through the spinach, discarding the garlic.

Serve a mound of warm spinach on each plate with the tomato perched on top.

Drizzle any remaining liquid over and serve.

*1 cup/8oz/250g uncooked rice = 3 cups/24oz/750g cooked rice.

Armenian Stuffed Tomato Salad

Ingredients

8 large, round tomatoes

4 tbsp olive oil

1 large onion, chopped finely

, large leek, green part removed and finely chopped

3 cups/24oz/750g steamed or boiled white or brown rice*

1/2 cup/4oz/125g toasted pine nuts

3/4 cup/6oz/175g currants

1/2 cup/4oz/125g parsley, chopped

1 tbsp fresh mint, chopped

3/4 tsp sea salt

1/2 tsp black pepper

2 cloves garlic, peeled and smashed

1/2 cup/4oz/125g vegetable stock

1/2 cup white wine

1lb/500g baby spinach leaves

Method

Boil the potatoes in their skins until just tender. Drain. Peel the potatoes while they are still hot and cut them into slices. Place them in a bowl with the onion.

Bring the stock to a boil with the vinegar. Once boiling, pour in the potatoes.

Leave to marinate until almost all the liquid is absorbed (about 20 minutes).

Pour off any excess liquid, then gently fold in the oil and mustard mixed together. Season with salt and pepper if necessary. Finally fold in the sour cream.

Serve at room temperature, garnished with dill or other fresh herbs.

German Potato Salad

Ingredients

6 medium potatoes

1 onion, finely chopped

¾ cup chicken stock

4 tbsp white vinegar

5 tbsp salad oil

2 tsp prepared German mustard

salt and freshly ground white pepper

1 cup sour cream

dill or other herbs to garnish

Method

Fill a large jug or bowl with hot water and immerse the rice noodles, allowing them to soak until soft, about 5-10 minutes. Drain and rinse under cold water to refresh, then place the noodles in a large mixing bowl.

Heat the olive oil in a small nonstick pan and add the ginger and chilies and sautè gently for a minute or two. Add the chopped peppers and raise the heat to medium high and stir-fry the pepper until softened. Add the spring onion slices and continue to cook for a further 2 minutes.

Tip the pepper mixture into the mixing bowl with the noodles and add the coriander, tossing thoroughly.

Whisk together the lime juice, rice vinegar, soy, and stock in a small jug and toss through the noodles. Sprinkle with the sesame seeds and chill before serving.

Ingredients

8oz/250g long, flat rice noodles	1/2 bunch coriander
1 tsp olive oil	juice of 1 lime
2 tsp freshly grated ginger	1 tbsp Japanese rice vinegar
1-2 small fresh red chilies, seeded and minced	1 tbsp soy sauce
1 red pepper, cut into small chunks	2 tbsp vegetable stock
6 shallots, sliced diagonally	3 tbsp sesame seeds

Japanese Rice Noodle Salad

Method

Shred the cabbage finely and transfer to a large mixing bowl. Thoroughly wash the bok choy, then slice them lengthways and add to the cabbage.

Wash the hallots then slice finely on the diagonal, and add to the cabbage mixture with the washed and roughly chopped coriander.

Toast the almonds and pine nuts Under the griller or in a dry frypan and set aside to cool. Alternatively, toast the nuts in a microwave by spreading the nuts over the microwave plate and cooking on HIGH for 2 minutes. Mix gently to distribute, then cook for consecutive extra minutes until the nuts are golden.

Allow to cool.

Mix the nuts and noodles with the cabbage salad.

To make the dressing: whisk all the ingredients together with a whisk until thick.

Drizzle over the salad and toss thoroughly then serve immediately.

Cabbage and Chinese Noodle Salad

Ingredients

Salad

½ curly green cabbage

4 baby bok choy

8 shallots

½ bunch fresh coriander

¾ cup/6oz/175g flaked almonds, toasted

½ cup/4oz/125g pine nuts, toasted

3½ oz/100g fried Chinese noodles

Dressing

4 tbsp peanut oil

2 tbsp balsamic vinegar

2 tbsp fresh lime or lemon juice

1 tbsp brown sugar (optional)

1 tbsp soy sauce

salt and cracked pepper to taste

Method

Cook the lentils in a saucepan of boiling water for 30 minutes or until tender.

Slice the top and bottom off each orange, using a small serrated knife—work over a bowl to catch the juices. Cut away the peel, following the curve of the fruit, then carefully cut between the membranes to release the segments. Squeeze the juice from the membranes into the bowl and reserve for the dressing. Arrange the watercress, orange segments, and smoked mackerel in serving bowls.

To make the dressing: mix together the horseradish, oil, seasoning and the reserved orange juice. Drain the lentils, stir into the dressing, then spoon over the salad and serve.

Ingredients

2oz/50g green lentils

4 small oranges

3oz/2 x 85g packs watercress

14oz/400g smoked mackerel fillet, skinned and

coarsely flaked

Dressing

4 tbsp horseradish cream

4 tbsp vegetable oil

salt and black pepper

Smoked Mackarel, Orange, and Lentil Salad

Method

To make the dressing: Place all the ingredients in a blender or food processor and blend until smooth. Set aside.

To make the salad: Heat oil in heavy medium saucepan over medium-high heat. Add a handful of tortilla strips and cook until crisp, about 4 minutes per batch, then remove from the oil and drain on absorbent paper.

Combine cabbage, lettuce, mango, jicama, onion, pepper, pumpkin seeds, and coriander in a large bowl. Toss with enough dressing to coat, adding salt and pepper to taste. Add the tortilla and serve.

Salad

oil for frying

4 corn tortillas, cut into strips

3 cups/1lb 11oz/750g thinly sliced green cabbage

3 cups/1lb 11oz/750g thinly sliced iceberg lettuce

1 mango, peeled and diced

1 cup/8oz/250g diced, peeled jicama

1 red or purple onion, finely diced

3 red peppers, roasted, peeled and sliced

1/2 cup/4oz/125g shelled pumpkin seeds, toasted

1/2 bunch coriander, chopped

salt and pepper to taste

Ingredients

Dressing

1 small mango, peeled, pitted, diced

1/2 cup grapefruit juice

1/4 cup fresh lime juice

1oz vegetable oil

1 clove garlic

1-2 small red chilies

4 shallots, chopped

Tortilla Salad Mexicana

salads

Method

Cook spirale (p. 14). Drain, rinse and leave to stand.

Melt the butter in a saucepan, add the lemon peel and juice. Stir to combine, then add the cream, herbs, chicken and spirale. Toss together lightly until heated through.

Spoon into a bowl, sprinkle with the Parmesan cheese and garnish with chives.

Serve as a warm salad with a separate bowl of tossed mixed lettuces.

Spirale with Chicken, Chives and Thyme

Ingredients

12oz/350 g spirale

2 tbsp snipped chives

2oz/60g butter

1 tbsp chopped thyme

grated peel of 1 lemon

3 cups/1lb/450g cooked chicken, chopped

4 tbsp lemon juice

½ cup/2oz/60g finely grated Parmesan cheese

1¼ cup light cream

chives, to garnish

Method

Place the onion, ginger, lemon juice and water in a food processor with the jogurt, spices and salt and process until the mixture is smooth. Remove from the processor and pour over the lamb cutlets, turning to coat both sides of the lamb. Marinate for a minimum of 4 hours or up to 8 hours.

Preheat the oven to 430°F/220°C. When you are ready to cook, mix the sesame seeds and onion seeds together and place them on a plate. Remove the lamb cutlets from the marinade one at a time, allowing the excess marinade to run off then dip each cutlet in the sesame mixture, coating both sides. Place the coated cutlets on a non-stick baking tray and bake in the preheated oven for 10 minutes for medium rare, or longer if desired.

Meanwhile, prepare the salad. Wash and dry the spinach and mixed lettuce leaves and place them, with the spring onions, in a large salad bowl. Whisk together the vinegar and oil with salt and pepper to taste then add the few drops of sesame oil, continuing to whisk until the dressing is thick. Toss the salad with the dressing until the leaves are well coated then divide the salad between 6 plates. Arrange 2 cutlets on each plate and serve immediately.

Black onion seeds (nigella) are available from Indian grocery stores. If unavailable, simply use extra sesame seeds.

Ingredients

Marinade

1 large onion, chopped	2 tsp ground cumin
⅔ oz/20g piece fresh ginger, grated	½ tsp ground turmeric
juice of 1 fresh lemon	¼ tsp cayenne
1 tbsp water	1 tbsp garam masala
½ cup plain jogurt	¼ tsp mace
2 tsp ground coriander	1 tsp salt

Tandoori Lamb Salad with Black Onion Seeds and Sesame

Salad

12 large lamb cutlets

1 cup sesame seeds

1/2 cup black onion seeds

8oz/250g baby spinach leaves

7oz/200g mesclun mix

4 shallots, sliced

3 tbsp white vinegar

1/4 cup peanut oil

few drops toasted sesame oil

salt and pepper to taste

Method

To make make the dressing: Whisk olive oil, lime juice, orange juice, soy sauce, rice vinegar, sesame oil, chives, and ginger in small bowl. Season with salt and pepper.

Heat a little oil in a frypan or wok and add the chili, spring onions, baby corn and snow peas, tossing over a high heat until the vegetables are crisp tender, about 3 minutes. Transfer the hot vegetables to a bowl and drizzle over a little of the dressing. Set aside.

Mix the sesame seeds and black onion seeds on a flat plate and season the fish with salt and pepper. Press the fish into the seed mixture, coating both sides evenly. Heat a little more oil in the same frypan used for the vegetables. Add the tuna and sear over a high heat until the fish is just cooked through. Transfer to a platter and, when cool, use a sharp knife to slice each fillet thinly.

To prepare the wontons: heat some vegetable oil in a wok or frypan and, when smoking, add the strips of wonton and cook until golden-brown. Remove from the pan and drain on paper towel. Add salt to taste.

Toss the lettuce leaves with the cooked vegetable mixture and a little more dressing, tossing thoroughly so that the leaves are well-coated. Add salt and pepper to taste. Divide the lettuce mixture between 4 plates and top with the sliced, seared tuna slices. Arrange a bundle of fried wonton strips on top.

Ingredients

Dressing

½ cup olive oil

¼ cup fresh lime juice

¼ cup orange juice

2 tbsp soy sauce

2 tbsp rice vinegar

1 tbsp toasted sesame oil

½ bunch fresh chives, minced

1 tbsp fresh ginger, minced

salt and pepper to taste

Seared Tuna Salad with Crisp Wontons

Salad

1-2 tbsp peanut oil

1 small red chili, minced

8 shallots, finely sliced on the diagonal

3½ oz/100g baby corn

5oz/150g snow peas, trimmed

4 tbsp/60g sesame seeds

4 tbsp black onion seeds (nigella)

4 x 5oz/150g tuna steaks

salt and pepper to taste

vegetable oil (for deep-frying)

8 wonton wrappers, cut into thin strips

8oz/250g mesclun mix

salads

83

Method

Place the chicken in a bowl, add the celery and walnuts and stir to mix. Core, and dice the apples, then toss in the lemon juice to keep from browning. Add to the chicken and mix well.

To make the dressing: mix together the mayonnaise, yogurt, lemon rind, and black pepper in a small bowl. Spoon over the chicken mixture and toss lightly to mix. Cover and refrigerate for at least 1 hour before serving.

Arrange the salad leaves on serving plates and spoon over the chicken mixture. Garnish with fresh chives.

Chicken Waldorf Salad

Ingredients

6oz/175g boneless chicken cooked breasts,

skinned and diced

4 sticks celery, thinly sliced

3oz/75g walnuts,

roughly chopped

1 red-skinned eating apple

1 green-skinned eating apple

juice of ½ lemon

7oz/200g bag mixed salad leaves

snipped fresh chives to garnish

Dressing

4 tbsp reduced calorie mayonnaise

4 tbsp low-fat natural yogurt

⅓ tsp finely grated lemon rind

black pepper

Method

Slice off the 2 fleshy sides of the mango close to the pit. Cut a criss-cross pattern across the flesh (but not the skin) of each side with a sharp knife. Push the skin inside out to expose the flesh and cut off the cubes. Place in a salad bowl with the salad leaves, sugar snap peas, and shallots, then toss together gently to mix.

To make the dressing: whisk together the olive oil, lime juice, honey, coriander and black pepper in a small bowl until thoroughly mixed.

Heat the sesame oil in a wok or large frying pan, add the duck and stir-fry over a high heat for 4-5 minutes until tender.

Add the warm duck to the mango salad, drizzle over the dressing, then toss together to mix. Garnish with fresh coriander.

Warm Duck and Mango Salad

Ingredients

1 ripe mango

4oz/125g mixed dark salad leaves such as

baby spinach, lollo rosso, and rocket

4oz/125g sugar snap peas, chopped

4 shallots, sliced diagonally

2 tsp sesame oil

8oz/225g boneless duck breast, skinned

and cut into strips

fresh coriander to garnish

Dressing

3 tbsp extra virgin olive oil

juice of 1/2 lime

1 tsp clear honey

2 tbsp chopped fresh coriander

black pepper

Method

Place the lima beans in a large bowl of warm water and soak overnight.

Drain the beans and place them in a saucepan of cold water. Bring to a boil and simmer for 1 hour or until just tender. Drain, reserving a ladle or two of the cooking water.

Heat the olive oil in a medium saucepan. Add the chili flakes and garlic, then sautè briefly until the garlic is golden. Add the prosciutto and stir over moderate heat until beginning to brown, about 2 minutes. Add the lima beans and cook, tossing occasionally, until heated through, about 3 minutes. Add some of the reserved cooking water if the mixture seems a little dry.

Season with salt and pepper and add the torn basil leaves and rocket. Toss gently then serve warm.

Ingredients

1lb/500g dried lima beans

2 tbsp olive oil

$\frac{1}{2}$ tsp dried chilli flakes

3 garlic cloves, minced

$3\frac{1}{2}$ oz/100g prosciutto, roughly chopped

salt and freshly ground pepper

10 basil leaves, torn

2 handfuls of rocket leaves or similar

Warm Lima Bean and Prosciutto Salad with Rocket

Method

To make the dressing: place the oil, vinegar, honey, and mustard in a cruet and shake well to combine.

Cook the pasta shells according to the packet instructions. When they are almost cooked, add the green beans and cook for 2 minutes or until the pasta is tender, but still firm to the bite and the beans have softened. Drain well.

Place the pasta and beans in a large bowl with the shallots, green pepper, cherry tomatoes, avocado, and seasoning. Add the dressing and toss well. Garnish with the basil.

Ingredients

6oz/175g dried pasta shells

5oz/150g fine green beans, halved

4 spring onions, sliced

1 green pepper, deseeded and chopped

4oz/125g cherry tomatoes, halved

1 large ripe avocado, halved, pittned and peeled

black pepper

torn fresh basil leaves to garnish

Dressing

3 tbsp olive or sunflower oil

1 tbsp white wine vinegar

1 tbsp clear honey

1 tsp Dijon mustard

Warm Mediterranean Pasta Shell Salad

Method

Slice the 4 sides off each pepper and discard the seeds.

Slice the pepper pieces into long, thin strips.

Heat the olive oil in a frypan and add the Spanish onion and rosemary and sauté on a high heat for 3 minutes. Add the garlic and all the pepper pieces, then toss thoroughly with the rosemary flavored oil.

Cook over a low heat for 30 minutes, stirring often until the pepper pieces are wilted and the onion has caramelised a little. Add the balsamic vinegar and cook for a further 5 minutes.

Add salt and pepper to taste and serve warm.

Ingredients

6 large pepper of assorted colors

2 tbsp virgin olive oil

1 large Spanish onion, peeled and cut into eights

3 tbsp fresh rosemary

3 cloves garlic, minced

1 tbsp balsamic vinegar

salt and freshly ground pepper to taste

Warm Salad of Pepper and Rosemary

Method

Heat the butter and olive oil in a large frypan and add the breadcrumbs, parsley, basil, and chives, then toss until golden. Add salt and pepper to taste.

Slice the tomatoes thickly and place them on a nonstick oven tray, adding salt and pepper to taste, then press the crumb mixture over the tomatoes to cover each slice.

Bake the tomatoes at 350°F/180°C for 10 minutes then grill just to toast the crumbs. Meanwhile, toss the lettuce leaves with the combined olive oil and vinegar and add salt and pepper to taste.

Arrange the lettuce leaves on a platter, then top with the tomato slices, allowing each to overlap the previous one. Grind fresh black pepper over and serve.

Ingredients

2 tbsp melted butter	salt and cracked black pepper to taste
2 tbsp olive oil	6-8 large tomatoes
2 cups fresh breadcrumbs	7oz/200g assorted mixed lettuce leaves
1/2 cup chopped parsley	2 tbsp olive oil
20 large basil leaves, finely sliced	1 tbsp balsamic vinegar
1/2 bunch chives, chopped	salt and pepper to taste

Warm Tomato Gratin Salad

Index